The Low Self-Esteem Struggle: Defeat Toxic Self-Criticism and Low Self-Worth

The Self Struggle, Volume 1

Scout Addison

Published by Scout Addison, 2023.

THE LOW SELF-ESTEEM STRUGGLE: DEFEAT TOXIC SELF-CRITICISM AND LOW SELF-WORTH

First edition. September 29, 2023.

Copyright © 2023 Scout Addison.

ISBN: 979-8223943457

Written by Scout Addison.

Table of Contents

<u>ScoutAddison.carrd.co</u>[1]

Cover designed by Getcovers

Preface

Self-esteem = how we value and perceive ourselves.

Throughout young adulthood and into my early thirties, I'd lived with a dire view of myself. I spoke poorly of myself, and not always just in my head, either; sometimes, my inner critic talked outwardly about how little I thought of myself.

I was so uncertain and unconfident in my decision-making abilities that I'd be engulfed in anxiety and panic should life require me to be assertive or confront a challenge. I would feel sick for weeks leading up to any kind of work or social gathering that I couldn't get out of, dreading having to talk to people who I was sure thought of me as dull, irritating, and unattractive. I felt entirely unlikeable and shunned many opportunities for decades, either not seeing them through the fog of my poor self-worth or shunning them for fear of (inevitable) rejection.

On the spectrum of self-esteem, I was a solid one out of ten - one feeling utterly devoid of worth, ten having a healthy view of oneself. From the age of around seven up to my mid-thirties, I endured life thinking I wasn't worthy. Note I didn't say I lived my life thinking I wasn't worthy: I endured it thinking it wasn't.

I was forever weathering the seemingly endless storm with no break from the relentlessness of the beating rain and thunder that was life. Before this, I was a pretty happy, easy-going child.

I was shy, and it took a little while for me to warm up to new people, but as a whole, life was good. I thought I was funny because all the adults told me so. I was a good little artist and frequently got praise for my drawings. As a whole, I liked being me.

Then, almost overnight, things changed. From six or seven upwards, my self-image declined rapidly, bouncing up and down as I went through my teens to taking a devastating dive when I hit 17. For the next 16 or so years, I struggled in every aspect of my life, with low self-esteem spearheading my poor mental health.

I treaded water career-wise because I didn't believe in myself enough to apply for promotions or seek work at a higher level. I felt so undeserving that I stayed in a toxic relationship for thirteen years. I would distance myself from any kind of connection and find myself in a position of spending many birthdays and holidays alone as a result. In short, I was a shell. I would worry, overthink, talk poorly about myself, and mull over events that had happened years ago. That was how I lived my life for such a long time, in my head and not in a good place at all.

I was triggered to confront this in my late thirties, which is still young, thankfully. Many people reach their eighties only to realize they've lived their entire lives this way, which only fuels their regret and pointless rumination in their twilight years. Since tackling my toxic thoughts and spending time battling them, I've found myself in a place of peace and contentment, a place bustling with self-worth.

I have not gone from introvert to extrovert, nor am I now a social butterfly.

I am, however, aware of my worth, and I work to enforce that in my day-to-day life. I no longer shun social events, and the notion of people thinking poorly of me no longer bothers me. I can look in the mirror and smile at the person looking back, safe in the knowledge that I'm full of strengths, quirks, kindness, and value. I make friends with great ease and have developed a few deep friendships since breaking down the barriers low self-esteem forces you to build up.

I'm now in a position that allows me more time to write, which I've always loved to do. It used to be short tales of fiction, then ghostwriting to running my blog (under a pseudonym). Part of me leveling up requires me to jump out of the comfort zone I'm currently in and allow myself to be more vulnerable. My idea is to merge my passion (writing) and my need to challenge myself (being vulnerable, open, and "putting myself out there") by creating a collection of books detailing my mental health struggles and explaining how those in a similar position can overcome them.

Low self-esteem, self-sabotage, lack of self-compassion, chronic overthinking... all of these things I call "*The Self Struggle.*"

Struggles most, if not all, of us have had to deal with at one point or another. The person I'm writing these books for, though, is the person who deals with these struggles on a long-standing basis. The person who, like me, found these struggles getting in the way of their lives, preventing them from happiness and fulfillment.

Over the years, I've kept handwritten diaries and journals, documenting how I felt and what I was struggling with at that time. Although the content in these journals is sporadic, it exposes just how low and miserable I was during that period.

Despite enduring and suffering from various mental well-being issues, I'd never made a coherent list of them until a few months ago. Instead of making me sad, it made me proud to see just how far I've come in a (relatively) short space of time. Most of the things on that list don't affect me anymore, and the ones that do are constantly kept in check by me and the systems I've put in place to manage them.

I want to reach as many people as possible, and I want these books to fall into the right hands. I'm opening up about my struggles to help you with yours. By no means am I a mental health professional, but I am someone who's been there. I've struggled with depression, negative self-talk, crippling anxiety, horrifically intrusive thoughts, and a plethora of other obstacles with my mental health, so if I can offer you some hope and light at the end of the tunnel, I want to do everything in my power to do so. I will tackle many book ideas this year, and I aim to create a library of resources for those struggling and, in turn, connect with them.

The Self Struggle is one you can overcome. You might not think it is possible just yet, but by the end of this book, my aim is not just for you to believe it's possible, but you'll know it's possible for *you*.

Before we begin, I'd like to be sure this book has found its way to someone who needs it. I understand you've picked it up because you feel you're struggling with self-esteem issues, but. I'd like to do a quick assessment with you to ensure you'll get value from this book.

I have five statements I'm going to give you, and I'd like you to answer them in one of four ways. You can firmly agree with the statement, agree with it, disagree with it, or firmly disagree.

Generally, I am satisfied with who I am.

I am a good source of encouragement for myself when things aren't going well.

I mostly feel like I'm a useful person.

My inner voice is generally kind and compassionate.

I don't find new situations to be a source of anxiety or unease.

If you found yourself disagreeing or firmly disagreeing with the above statements, that's a strong indicator that this book has found its way to someone who needs it. If you've agreed or firmly agreed to the above statements, I believe you don't need this book. You may put it back on the shelf, but of course, you may continue reading if you feel you or someone you love needs it.

This book is laid out in five stages:

Stage One: Understanding low self-esteem.

Stage Two: Finding the cause of your low self-worth.

Stage Three: Overcoming your toxic inner critic.

Stage Four: Conquering blame, shame, and guilt.

Stage Five: Dealing with negative social comparison.

Stage Six: Being assertive without the aftermath of guilt.

If you've decided this is the book for you, let's begin dissecting and dismantling the low self-esteem struggle. After all, life is far too short to live with low self-esteem.

The Surefire Signs of Low Self-Esteem

This is Stage One of your journey toward self-worth: understanding what low self-esteem is.

Now, you're reading this, so you know you're struggling with your self-esteem. (Believe it or not, this is a good starting point. Many people won't acknowledge their self-esteem struggle, instead believing it's just a part of their personality. Remember, low self-esteem is not a personality trait.)

I'm going to granulate self-esteem into six symptoms. It's a broad phrase to suffer from "low self-esteem." I want to help you clarify and process exactly what that means for you.

I want to validate your genuine struggle with esteem by outlining what you and millions of others are enduring daily. It's always reassuring to read about the symptoms of poor self-esteem and go, "Me too... I do that... I feel that... and that," as you read the expansive list of low self-esteem signs. It makes you feel less isolated with your feelings. With the byproducts of low self-esteem that I'll cover in this chapter, I'll also add my own experiences and challenges here and there.

The aim of this chapter is for you to grasp the symptoms of your low self-worth fully. Sometimes, we just need someone else to hold these things in front of our face to fully process and accept them. Once you fully understand the negative symptoms of low self-esteem, you can make your way to Stage

Two: understanding what caused your low self-worth. I'll give you a hint: none of us are born with low self-esteem. We're molded into disliking ourselves by others.

You may be tempted to dive straight into Stage Two. You can if you want to, that's fine, but I'd suggest working through this chapter first. You may say, "I already know what low self-esteem is - I live with it daily!" This is a valid point. But this chapter will thoroughly dissect the symptoms of low self-esteem and help you get a clearer picture of what you're up against. In order to slay the demon, you need to understand it, and that's what these first two chapters will help you do.

Low Self-Esteem Symptom #1: Toxic Comparisons

We're humans; we all do it. We naturally compare ourselves to peers, friends, work colleagues, and people off TV. Whereas a healthy mind will make the comparison, acknowledge it, and move on, someone with low self-esteem will compare themselves relentlessly to others in a horribly unhealthy way. Someone with a healthy dose of self-perception may use that comparison with another to improve certain aspects of themselves. For example, they may see their friend run a marathon which inspires them to start training to partake in an upcoming run.

The social comparison here would be toxic rather than motivational for someone with poor self-esteem. They may use this as a way to provoke some poisonous self-talk. They may feel "lesser than" the person running the marathon and feel inadequate around them. This is sometimes referred to as "upward social comparison." We all engage in it, but it's essential to make sure we check ourselves before our self-esteem makes it a toxic trait, but more on that later in the book.

Social media is a cesspool of filters, movie star lifestyles, flash cars, and perfect homes. This makes it an ideal incubator for toxic comparisons. It's not just famous people we make unfair comparisons to, either.

I would obsess over the social media profile of a girl I went to school with, eager to see how much further her career was than mine. Even though we'd been in the same field as each other for ten years, she was much more senior than me. She'd climbed the ladder much more rapidly than me and was clearly earning double my salary, judging by the lavish holidays she'd go on and the fancy restaurants she'd always seem to be in.

We embarked on the same career path at precisely the same time, yet she was so much further ahead of me. More than that, socially, she was a butterfly, effortlessly gliding from my dream job to my dream social circle in each post she made. I'd look at her profile, not to see what she'd done differently to me and try to get inspiration from her to better my life but rather to feed my low self-esteem and confirm what I already knew: that I was a second-class individual in comparison.

Of course, now I know those thoughts are nothing but toxic concepts I would peddle into reality, but they were my truth at the time. I would compare myself in such a horrific way that, in the end, I would feel anxious at the thought of her profile coming up on my social media feed, knowing it would make me dissolve into a pit of worthlessness.

And, to reconfirm just how much social media only shows the highlights of people's lives, it turned out the friend I was comparing myself to had been dealing with her own battles behind her picture-perfect online life. Her relationship was breaking down, and she'd been dealing with family issues all the while I was scrolling her feed and berating myself for not being her. I felt so stupid and self-obsessed when I got a glimpse beneath the veneer of her picture-perfect life.

It reinforced the old saying that you should always be kind since you never know what others may be going through. It also reinforced that social media is a conveyor belt of "wonderful life" lies that should be viewed cautiously.

Do you find yourself doing this? Your situation may differ from my example, but that's one of many I have. From my pretty sister to my rich cousins, I constantly compared myself so harshly and unjustly. For you, it may be a coworker, a sister-in-law, or even a celebrity. It doesn't matter who it is; the feelings are still the same. The toxic comparison will always leave you feeling less than and paltry. But the ironic thing is you're not. Another adage comes to mind, a quote from Einstein: *if you judge a fish by its ability to climb trees, it will go through its whole life believing that it's stupid.*

Low Self-Esteem Symptom #2: Toxic Self-Talk

"I'm so stupid!"

"I can't do anything right."

"No wonder I don't have many friends."

"I'll never be good enough to land my dream job."

"I'm so unattractive; no one will ever want me."

This kind of self-talk goes far beyond the rumination of your inner critic. It serves no beneficial purpose other than to keep you feeling low and stressed out and to ensure your self-confidence remains at hazardous levels.

One dangerous thing about low self-esteem is that negative self-talk can often creep up covertly and engulf your thoughts to the point that it becomes the norm. You may think to yourself, "I think I'll skip the gym this morning. I've left it too late, and now it'll be busy. I might not get to use the equipment I want. I'll go later in the evening."

While this may be true, for people with poor self-perception, this seemingly innocent comment may be masking the real reason for not wanting to go to the gym. Insecurity and the thoughts of being looked at and judged in a crowded gym are off-putting, and the idea of exposing yourself in such a vulnerable way is too daunting to handle. But, your negative thinking of yourself has become so ingrained into your daily life that it can be hard to differentiate normal thinking from derogatory thinking.

Low self-esteem often causes outright cruel and nasty self-talk, filled with words of blame and feelings of disdain. I'll cover this aspect of low self-esteem in more depth in Stage Three.

Low Self-Esteem Symptom #3: Insecurity and Self-Doubt

When our self-worth is low, we don't readily accept that we can make good choices. We can't make the right decision because we don't trust our judgment. In some cases, we freeze and look to others to guide our way for us. This was true for me, and sometimes, this led to me being given (and acting upon) poor advice that wasn't always in my best interests.

The insecurity and self-doubt you feel causes issues in just about every aspect of your life. You have doubts about the strength of your relationship. If you're single, you doubt your worthiness of being in a happy relationship. You doubt your skills, your intelligence, your decision-making, and your intuition.

Our intuition is an innate part of who we are as a person. When you don't trust your instincts, how can you have a healthy sense of self?

Insecurity shows itself as a persistent feeling of inadequacy. It hangs over you like a cloud, following your every move. You simply do not feel good enough for just about anything. You may feel undeserving of your relationship. You may feel undeserving of love. Should someone compliment you or your skills, you may feel as if it's out of pity or even a cruel joke. Even kindness is something you feel undeserving of. Has someone ever gone out of their way for you or even just done something kind for you, and it's made you feel bad because you don't feel worthy of such considerate treatment?

If so, you're not alone. These persistent feelings of insecurity cause a plethora of its own symptoms. This general uncertainty about the world affects your relationships and your ability to open up and talk and hinders your communication skills. As a result, you're often left feeling misunderstood, and your wants and needs remain unmet.

Low Self-Esteem Symptom #4: Self-Neglect

"Self-care" is a relatively new phrase coined to describe the act of overseeing your own mental, physical, and emotional well-being. The recent avalanche of self-help fads and trends has seen self-care become a basic requirement in your self-worth toolkit.

Unlike many of these fads, which can spew woo-woo tips and advice, self-care is essential to living a fulfilled life. I don't say that lightly, either. I'm a big supporter of self-help content, but even I have to admit, you do need to wade through a lot of dubious material before you find the good stuff. The connection between self-care and your mental health is indisputable.

When you suffer from low self-esteem, practicing self-care just isn't feasible. If it is, it's sporadic. In fact, poor esteem, more often than not, equals self-neglect.

This can mean you are hit-and-miss with your hygiene from time to time. Sometimes, it's just too much to get clean, and even though you know you'd feel much better after a warm shower, clean hair, and fresh clothing, the task feels too hard to complete. If you feel like this regularly, you might sometimes call yourself lazy or slothful. Please know that you're neither of those things: you're dealing with low self-esteem, a debilitating pattern of thinking that prevents you from carrying out simple self-care duties without a struggle.

It's not just hygiene that's affected either. Your day-to-day duties can often be neglected too, tasks that may not seem big to those on the outside looking in but feel insurmountable to you. For example, say you need to phone the bank to rectify an issue with your account. You know they open at eight and close at six; you know what you need to say when you call up.

But you keep putting it off. You bury the thought of the task until you forget about it. Until, of course, you remember you need to call the bank, and the idea makes you freeze in your tracks. "I'll do it tomorrow" or "I'll try to email them later" might help you shrug off the niggling thought that you need to complete this task. But the call doesn't happen when tomorrow comes, and the small task snowballs into a bigger issue.

I'll take this moment to check in and ask if you have a to-do list. If so - and it's a great idea to have one - what's on the top of it? Why don't you put this book down and go cross it off? I'll be here when you get back. You'll feel much better if you go get it done, whatever it is. If you don't have a list, do you have anything niggling you know you need to get done but have been putting off? Now's your chance to go get it crossed off.

I used to deal with self-neglect and struggled to carry out day-to-day tasks. The call to the bank I referenced would be something that would cause me anxiety. I'd put it off and put it off until, eventually, the bank would end up calling *me*. I wound up in debt because I neglected to pay bills. My mail piled up next to my front door. Phone calls went unanswered. I just shut down.

To someone with a healthy relationship with themselves, they'd pull their boots up, head to the pile of mail stacking up, open each one, and read the contents. Once they'd processed what the mail was - an overdue bill, a credit card statement, a reminder that the dog is due a vet appointment, or to advise them the price of Wi-Fi is going up - they'd set the letter in front of them and deal with it.

They'd pay the bill. They'd book the dog in for their appointment. They'd ring their Wi-Fi provider to secure a better deal. Combining all of these tasks wouldn't take too much time to complete. And once they're done, they're done. But, when we're dealing with a poor perception of ourselves, we aren't thinking with a healthy mind. As a result, many "basic" tasks get put off as they feel too difficult to tackle.

You may know as much as I do that this inaction just breeds an even worse view of ourselves. We know what we need to do - be it flossing our teeth, taking the bins out, returning a call, or doing some washing - but are unable to do so.

If you struggle with this regularly or intermittently, you may have been called idle or lazy by those around you. Understandably, you'd take this to heart and believe it even. But, it's a symptom of what's going on inside your head, an outward reflection of your inner turmoil.

Don't feed your negative self-talk by dwelling on this. We'll work on all your symptoms throughout this book. You're working on your self-esteem, which will positively impact all the symptoms it causes. You're reading this book, you're taking strides to overcome the fog in your mind, and for that, you should feel a sense of pride.

Low Self-Esteem Symptom #5: Guilt and Shame

If there was a super-fuel for low self-esteem, it's feelings of guilt and shame. If any emotions can keep us in a state of suppression, poor self-image, and unhappiness, it's the combination of guilt and shame.

The word "guilt" suggests you have done something to feel guilty about. You haven't.

With esteem issues, the guilt we feel is simply for not being good enough. Not attractive enough, not smart enough, not successful enough, or not funny enough. We feel guilt for merely being ourselves. Who we are brings us shame. This combo keeps us awake at night, ruminating over what other people think of us. The guilt of not being enough and the shame of everyone seeing and knowing this can be all-encompassing.

I've wasted many a good night's sleep by lying awake, guilt keeping me from my slumber, berating myself for being so useless.

Recalling how I used to view myself makes me feel compassion for my former self. If I could go back in time, I'd be able to comfort my past self. To tell her it's going to be okay, that these feelings aren't real. The things I'm agonizing over and feeling shame about don't matter. I'd tell her these feelings of shame and guilt were bestowed upon her during her childhood and not only remained with her into adulthood but took over her sense of self.

These feelings stop us from living. We don't dare try to be or do more; shame takes care of that. *How dare we think we can do better?!*

The difficult thing is articulating this feeling to other people. I remember trying to explain these persistent feelings of guilt to someone I knew, and their response was, "Just stop overthinking." They meant well, but their response was akin to being told to stop being anxious when you're feeling anxious. All it does is make you feel alone in your feelings and reinforce that nobody can help drag you out of these low times.

There *is* someone who can drag you from the pits of low self-esteem. And by the end of this book, you will know who that is, how they can do it, and be entirely confident they can do it.

Low Self-Esteem Symptom #6: Rejection Sensitive Dysphoria

You may not have heard of rejection-sensitive dysphoria before. It's not as clinical as it sounds, though. It's a term used to describe your discomfort with rejection or putting yourself in situations where you may be rejected.

Granted, none of us like rejection, but when you suffer from rejection sensitivity, it becomes overwhelmingly painful to put yourself in situations that might provoke those feelings.

Those who endure RSD find it difficult to process the negative emotions that follow a rejection. They simply can't manage it. They may even have those gut-churning feelings of rejection where there wasn't a rejection in the interaction; it's just the sufferer's interpretation.

Do you feel anxious and panicked when you're in a situation that might result in something you perceive to be a rejection? If the interaction ends up being something you believe to be a rejection, how do you react? Do you have a knee-jerk reaction? Do negative emotions like rage, extraordinary anxiety, and intense sadness envelop you? If so, you could be enduring rejection-sensitive dysphoria.

The impact of dealing with this is twofold. Not only are you in a state of unease and discomfort when you're faced with a situation that might end in rejection, you also struggle to handle the perceived rejection in a healthy way.

For example, you could have a meeting with your boss. They may pinpoint some key areas you can improve upon in your job. A person with a healthy view of oneself would take this feedback on board, push back on areas they feel their boss is incorrect, and engage with them to move forward in their role.

A person with an unhealthy view of themselves, who deals with rejection sensitivity, may see this feedback from their boss as a personal attack. The words and phrases their boss uses may feel like a punch to the stomach. The overwhelming emotional pain of this perceived rejection - not being good enough - sets off a domino effect of negative emotions. RSD is a common trigger for negative self-talk, which perpetuates the whole toxic cycle of low self-esteem.

The feelings soon become embarrassment, a lesser-known aspect of dealing with low self-esteem. We find ourselves feeling humiliated incredibly easily, and although we do our best to contain this melting pot of negativity, sometimes we simply can't. We react, our emotions bursting out uncontrollably. This may be crying, showing anger, or taking off from the situation. Our knee-jerk reaction often proves later on to be another source of embarrassment.

But why are we so sensitive to rejection? What is it about this very normal aspect of life that we find so difficult to deal with?

There are two main reasons, although you may find that both apply to you:

You're a people pleaser, a trait you learned to survive childhood. Rejection brings back the horrible feelings you felt, and you want to avoid this at all costs.

You already feel like a failure. Rejection validates this negative view of yourself, and you want to avoid this at all costs.

These are the six symptoms of low self-esteem. Some of these may be familiar - too familiar - for you. You may have been suffering some of these symptoms but just hadn't pinpointed them or been able to put a name to the feeling. This is why I feel this first chapter is important - you have to understand the beast you're battling.

But just as important is reverse engineering. The goal is for you to have a healthy view of yourself, a healthy dose of self-esteem, and to hold yourself in positive regard. After all, if you don't hold yourself in high regard, you put that negative image of yourself out into the world, which people pick up on. If you can't champion yourself, who will?

Back to reverse engineering. So, we understand the way in which your low self-esteem manifests itself. Now, we need to look at high self-esteem.

Too many people think having high esteem for yourself is bad, vain, and egotistical. It's not. It's not loving every inch of yourself and denouncing every person who doesn't love every bit of you. It's not having a narcissistic view of yourself or having unwavering confidence. It's not arrogance or pretentiousness.

High self-esteem is regarding yourself as worthy. It's holding yourself in positive regard. It's not putting yourself down; it's offering yourself compassion and empathy; it's avoiding toxic self-talk and a frame of mind that lets you live without self-loathing.

Of course, even those with a healthy view of themselves have bad days. They find themselves in situations that may cause embarrassment or do things they wish they hadn't. The difference is that they don't let these things consume them. Mistakes don't define them. A blip in their day doesn't ruin their day or week; it's just that, a blip. They have a healthy amount of respect for the way they speak to themselves. They're able to silence the inner critic when they try spouting their toxic talk. They can rationalize interactions with others and avoid overthinking situations that cause embarrassment.

Those with high self-esteem don't take things personally. They see the bigger picture; they don't live their lives in the insular, reclusive way those with low self-esteem can so often do. They know they have a deserving place in this world.

By the end of this book, there are four key aspects that I want you to be challenging:

The regard in which you hold yourself.

Keeping challenges in perspective.

How you talk to yourself.

How you deal with difficult feelings toward yourself.

This is the end of Stage One. As a quick recap, these are the six major symptoms of low self-esteem:

Toxic Comparisons

Toxic Self-Talk

Insecurity and Self-doubt

Self-Neglect

Guilt and Shame

Rejection Sensitive Dysphoria

Now we can move on to Stage Two: getting to the root cause of your low self-esteem. Before we do, if you can, list events or situations where the above symptoms have reared their heads. Specific times your low self-esteem has made you feel guilt, shame, or insecurity. Events that have caused you to fear rejection or situations where you've had to face a perceived rejection and note your reaction to that. Times when paranoia has overwhelmed you. Periods where your self-care has dissolved into self-neglect. For each symptom, write down a memorable episode of that manifesting itself.

Either use a notes app on your phone or paper if you have some handy. We'll come back to it later.

What Causes Low Self-Esteem?

There's no one reason that some people suffer from low self-esteem. For each of us who have poor self-perception, we all have different reasons why we feel that way about ourselves. Still, these reasons can often fit into similar origin stories. Nobody is born with low self-esteem; it's something we develop from our interactions with others. This is a sad truth we have to confront when tackling our issues with esteem.

If you delve into your relationships - past and/or present - you will often find the source of your low self-esteem. Over time, the way we view ourselves manifests into something so cruel and deafening that we forget where our ugly view of ourselves was born. After all, it didn't just appear out of nowhere suddenly.

These relationships that founded our toxic thoughts about ourselves could be a parental/caregiver one, a past romantic relationship, a present partner, or a traumatic experience with peers at school (such as being bullied or unable to make friends).

When I wanted to face my low self-esteem, one of the first things I had to do, aside from acknowledging it, was try and discover the source of it. When did it start, and why? As someone who used to purposefully suppress traumatic or shameful memories, it was a struggle. A lot of my childhood had been blanked out by me as a coping mechanism. I had to face some demons, and I had to force myself to see this search through until the end, even if it meant facing traumatic experiences head-on.

What I discovered in my search was that suppression is far, far worse than facing horrible memories. You may not believe that right now, but once you're out on the other side, you'll understand what I mean.

It turned out my low self-esteem originated from my mother's emotional abuse of me. I'll explain a little more about this throughout the chapter, but what I'd called a "strained" relationship for so long turned out to be a rather abusive one. During my search for answers, I was overwhelmed by the number of people who have also been negatively affected by their relationship with their caregivers or parental figures.

It made me do a deep dive into the correlation between low self-esteem and parents, and it was like a light went on for me. Despite confronting difficult memories, I was happy to be finding the reason for my thoughts to rectify them.

This chapter is intended to explain your low sense of self by outlining the common causes of poor self-esteem. The next step, after delving into the cause, is to confront it, understand it, and rationalize it - but I won't get ahead of myself. For now, let's look over the four common reasons for low self-esteem. You may find your poor self-image is a result of a number of these root causes merged, or you may just have one root cause. Either way, by delving into the origins of your lack of worth, we can work to overcome it.

Root of Low Self-Esteem #1: Abuse From Parental Figure(s)

Emotional and/or physical abuse from your caregiver when you're a child is undeniably a traumatic experience. When the very people entrusted to take care of our well-being, both emotional and physical, end up abusing that trust and mistreat us, our view of the world naturally changes.

Verbal abuse, emotional neglect, harsh punishment, and physical harm are all powerful things to endure. Children who experience these things consistently will undoubtedly believe they're experiencing these things because they are bad, unworthy, and deserving of such treatment.

This lack of self-worth doesn't just vanish once the child grows up and leaves home. It stays with them into adulthood, affecting their adult relationships, their ability to give and receive warmth and affection, and their ability to communicate effectively with others.

Growing up in a chaotic home, like I did, where encouragement and praise weren't given freely, or barely at all, erodes your self-worth. A child living in a state of fear, always worried about how they're going to upset their parents, breeds a timid, unworthy view of themselves.

I was always anxious as to how I would enrage my mother next. If she gave me the job of dusting the ornaments in the living room, I'd freeze in fear of how she'd react if I didn't do it right. If I used too much polish. If I didn't put the ornaments back in the right place. If I took too long to do it. I couldn't just get on with the task and report back to my mother once I'd done it; I'd learned from prior experience it wouldn't be that easy. She'd inspect my work, and if I'd done something incorrectly, I'd be made to feel useless.

Sometimes, she'd call me stupid for my inability to do things. Sometimes, she'd passively aggressively sigh without outright reprimanding me for my misgivings. But, I'd know I ought to feel shame and guilt for not being good enough. Even from a young age, I remember getting the flushes of self-loathing as she shouted at me for spilling a drink or being clumsy. Tears would well up, my face would burn from the inner turmoil brewing, and I'd feel like the most worthless person on the planet.

Of course, there were times when my mother did show maternal elements. Often, this was in front of others, a front perhaps. Still, because of how utterly worthless and stupid she'd made me feel time after time, when she did bestow me with some form of kindness, I'd feel undeserving of it.

Like when I got what I asked for at Christmas or when she brought me a bar of chocolate back from her shopping trip. Or that time she ruffled my hair as I sat watching TV; the unexpected show of affection came out of nowhere, and although it was something I craved, it was also something that made me feel awkward and uneasy. I didn't feel like I deserved to be given that kind of attention since I often disappointed her.

As I grew up, these feelings grew too and would affect my adult relationships. I didn't reconcile the connection between my low self-esteem and my mother's treatment of me for such a long time, but once I did, I was able to connect all my negative adult thoughts of myself to their childhood origins.

Without positive reinforcement, a child becomes incredibly uncertain of themselves. When you add in emotional abuse and conditional love, the cruel parent essentially creates a young human lacking in self-esteem. Whether that's their intention or not is irrelevant; their toxic behavior molds their child's view of themselves and stays with them until they're in a position to confront it - often decades later.

The thing about being a survivor of trauma is that even though we didn't cause the damage, it's our job to fix it. For a while, I was resentful of this fact. I didn't cause my low self-worth or the lack of respect I had for myself, but I had to be the one to amend that. I was the one left with that task, not the person who'd carried out the mistreatment of me.

This way of thinking, despite so many of us thinking this way, is a victim's mentality. It will keep us in the pits of low self-esteem. We must take accountability for our own mental well-being. I agree - it's not fair. But, it puts the power back in our hands.

Think back to your childhood. In just about every case of low self-esteem, this is where the insecurities begin. Do you recall your parents making you feel as if you weren't good enough? Like you were a burden or unwanted? Did you ever feel like your presence was merely tolerated? Do you recall particularly hurtful things your caregiver said to you and how their words stung, so much so that when you think about them now, you still wince?

Perhaps you had a sibling who was more intelligent than you, and their academic skills were held over you and used to make you feel stupid. Your parents would compare you unfavorably to your brother or sister, and feelings of resentment and self-loathing would fester within you.

In many instances of childhood mistreatment, the parent - often a narcissistic parent - will place their own wants and needs before their children's. This doesn't go unnoticed by the child, either. It's quickly picked up on, and the youngster will do their best to meet the (often unattainable) desires of their parent. The people-pleasing child will do everything within their power to keep on the "good side" of their parent, essentially doing so to avoid maltreatment.

Often, this will cause something called "self-erasure" - the child, desperate for acceptance and love from their parent, will neglect their own wants and needs in order to bend to give their parent what they want. The child is unable to say no to their parent, something that almost always follows them into adulthood. This loss of self the child puts themselves through simply in order to survive also remains.

If your lack of self-esteem began in childhood, I want you to refer back to the notes you made from chapter one, where you noted down specific times your low self-esteem has made you feel guilt, shame, or insecurity; events where you can vividly recall the symptoms rearing their heads.

Now, refer back to the terrible feelings you had in that situation. Whether it be crushing embarrassment, overwhelming shame, or immense feelings of inadequacy, I want you to harness that feeling. I know you might think this is counterintuitive, asking you to put yourself back in that dreadful feeling but bear with me.

Now, with that negative emotion, I want you to revert to your childhood and see yourself feeling that emotion as a child. It should take you back to a specific scenario. What is the scenario you've returned to? Perhaps you're being verbally abused by your mother and feel burning embarrassment because she's doing it in front of other family members. Perhaps you've been taken back to a time when a parent was giving you the silent treatment, and you are left with intense insecurity since you're unsure what you've done wrong.

Maybe you're seven years old, and you're drowning in shame after you accidentally overheard your mother blaming your father for you being so "funny looking." This happened to me, and I recall it vividly. It was the first time I'd considered how I looked. I wasn't bothered too much before, but after hearing that, I took myself to the bathroom, stared in the mirror, and picked myself apart. This would be a habit that would stay with me for almost three decades.

The point of this exercise is to create a thread from the toxic thoughts you have of yourself as an adult and follow it back to its childhood origin. It might take some time and thought, but follow that invisible thread and make the connection.

It could be that your self-esteem issues weren't caused by mistreatment from your caregivers, but the idea remains the same: take the negative feeling you have as an adult and retrace it back to your earliest memory of it. With that in mind, let's cover the second reason we end up with a dire view of ourselves.

Root of Low Self-Esteem #2: Bullying or the Inability to "Fit In"

Those who suffered bullying as a child can attest to how deep the scars go. The cutting insults, the isolation, the physical torment, and the lack of anyone stepping in to help you are hard memories to rehash. Sadly, the after-effects of bullying last a long time after you escape your tormentors. One of the long-standing effects of bullying is low self-esteem.

While enduring bullying and thereafter, the self-loathing and seclusion you feel makes it hard to make friends. If anyone should express an interest in being your friend, you feel like they're either doing it to trick you or as some kind of favor out of pity. To have to feel this way throughout school or in your workplace only serves to reaffirm what the bullies were telling you: you're unimportant. Worthless. Of course, these toxic thoughts aren't true, but when you've endured enough experiences that tell you that you are, you begin to accept it as the truth.

Perhaps you had supportive parents during this traumatic period. Maybe you didn't. Regardless, the distress you endured would remain the same. Still, the way your caregivers reacted during this time would determine what kind of impact the bullying had on you.

If your parents were uninterested or uninvolved, of course, this would have made you feel as if you were undeserving of being advocated for. They didn't step in because they didn't care enough to see what was going on. Should you have told your parents about issues with bullying and were dismissed or told to tell a teacher or use violence as a retort, then this would have left you feeling utterly hopeless. As you may know, hopelessness is a constant when you feel devoid of self-worth.

As a result, you'd retreat further into your shell and hope to become invisible to all the predatory people and cruel tormentors who used you to make themselves feel a sense of power and dominance.

Perhaps your parents were involved and wanted to support you during this time. This, of course, gives you a higher possibility of fully recovering from the trauma of bullying since you feel cared for. However, sometimes parents can be too involved, trying to quash their child's awful experience by overly invasive tactics. This can cause the child to refrain from going to their parents for help, perhaps lying about or downplaying the level of bullying taking place. Again, this leads to the child feeling alone, isolated, and dealing with a traumatic experience without help.

If your parents paint you as a victim, then that's how you begin to see yourself.

Low self-esteem can also be born without the presence of bullying during childhood. Maybe you weren't bullied or hounded by your peers, but you still weren't able to "fit in." Either you couldn't find a crowd that resonated with you, or the people you wanted to befriend simply didn't let you join their circle. You were a loner, someone who struggled to slot into the societal puzzle pieces you were "supposed" to fit into.

This would make you feel different, less than, and alone. When you're a child and left dealing with these feelings without anybody to reach out to for support, they end up manifesting until your sense of self is distorted. Before long, it becomes low self-esteem.

I was somewhat of a loner in school. I didn't have a solid group of friends. In fact, from the ages of 12 - 15, I flitted from group to group, never really being a major member of any of them. In between being part of a group, my school lunchtimes were spent in the library, using the computers until it was time to head back to class. I had huge friendship insecurity, and although I wasn't explicitly bullied, I struggled to find and keep friends. This made me feel like I wasn't worthy of having friends, and each time I invariably fell out of favor with whatever group I tried to befriend, it hit me like a punch in the stomach.

This inability to make friends, for me, began with my mother's mistreatment of me. So, I don't believe my lack of self-esteem was born from not fitting in, but it certainly was exacerbated by it.

Again, if you had a traumatic time with bullying or not fitting in, I want you to refer back to your notes of specific times your low self-esteem has made you feel guilt, shame, embarrassment, or rejection. Can you retrace that feeling back to childhood? Perhaps your perpetual feelings of shame are rooted in a particularly nasty bullying incident from your youth. Maybe your constant shame and embarrassment began the day you tried to confide in someone about the bullying, only to be made to feel stupid for reaching out. Tie your current symptoms of low self-esteem to their historical origins, and take some time to reconcile that.

In doing so, you'll find a newfound sense of compassion for yourself.

Root of Low Self-Esteem #3: Mistreatment From a Partner

Being involved with an abusive partner will erode your self-esteem quicker than you can realize what's going on. Often, because those of us with a poor view of ourselves don't feel deserving of true love, we'll enter a relationship with someone who mistreats us and endure their abuse because we don't know any different. However, sometimes, we enter a relationship with a healthy view of ourselves, and by the end of it, we are a shell of our former selves. The trauma we endure at the hands of a lover displaces everything we think about ourselves and our worth.

Initially, I entitled this subsection "Domestic Abuse." However, "Mistreatment From a Partner" is a much more accurate descriptor for this root of low self-esteem. When you hear the term "domestic abuse," many of us jump to images of violent episodes or the victim enduring beating after beating. Abusive relationships are much broader than this, and "abuse" is an umbrella term for much more than violence.

It's verbal abuse. It's persistent lying from your spouse. It's gaslighting. It's tireless put-downs. It's feeling emotionally unsafe. It's the fear of upsetting them. It's being threatened. It's cheating, emotional or physical. It's a power imbalance. It's being ridiculed under the guise of "jokes." It's being blamed for anything and everything that goes wrong.

Of course, just about every abusive relationship doesn't begin this way. It begins as you'd expect, perhaps with the addition of being "love bombed." You may be blindsided by this person who acts as if they adore you like they think you ought to be together, and like they can't be without you.

But, before long, things turn bad. The once adoring love interest is now easy to anger, moody a lot of the time, and almost treats you with resentment. It could take weeks for things to turn sour, or often, it happens months down the line. Either way, the abuse begins little by little. Small blips begin to become more frequent, your partner's jealousy becomes more apparent, and they begin to question your whereabouts or consider your honesty.

Some of these abusive traits can initially come across as a sign of affection. Jealousy can come across like your partner is afraid to lose you. Wanting to know where you are all the time can feel like they care for your safety. In reality, they're beginning to exert control and dominance over you.

The point of manipulation is the victim is unaware they're being manipulated. Abusers are masters at executing this form of abuse seamlessly, and before we know it, we're left feeling insecure, full of doubt, and full of blame for the downward turn the relationship has taken. This instability in our lives, seemingly caused by us, leaves us with disdain for ourselves. We try to claw back what we had before: the love our partner used to give us, the safety we felt with them, and a life without fear. This desperation often leads to rejection, further fueling our low self-worth.

Unbeknown to us, while we're enduring it, this is exactly the hellish place the abuser wants us in. To be fuzzy-headed, unsure of ourselves, desperate for their love. Our despair tightens the control they have over us.

One of the main questions a victim of abuse often gets when they flee their abuser is, "Why did it take you so long to leave?" It is a misguided, insensitive question that exposes how little people know about the connection between abuse and low self-esteem.

Those with low self-worth have shame coursing through their veins. And what helps shame multiply? Secrecy, silence, and fear of judgment. The first two are enforced by the abuser, and they ensure the victim doesn't speak up, or else feel the ultimate shame of being judged. Even in today's world, victims of abuse are shamed for "staying so long," "not seeking help," or "letting someone treat them that way." While abuse is never the victim's shame to bear, far too often, they're made to hold that weight on their shoulders. It's a vicious cycle for the person enduring it.

For those of us whose esteem was crushed during childhood, by the time we enter adulthood, we're in a more vulnerable position when dating possible abusers. That's not to say every person who endured trauma as a child goes on to be abused by their spouse, but you may know yourself when your esteem is low, you tend to put up with a lot more than someone with a healthy view of themselves. As a result, we can find ourselves in partnerships - a term I use loosely here - with people who only serve to erode our self-esteem further.

In instances like this, if you open yourself up and let your spouse know about your past traumas and painful memories, your partner may use this against you. They know your triggers, the things that can break you, and the vulnerabilities you have. An abusive, manipulative individual would use these to their nefarious advantage to retain control over you.

You drown in thoughts of worthlessness and self-hatred. Here's the crux - despite all your "bad points" and "flaws," you still have that one person by your side - your spouse. Even though they put you through hell and are potentially the source of your low self-esteem, you don't add up all the dots. Your mind is so clouded by self-loathing that you can't rationalize this. You can't compute that the source of your comfort is also the source of your inner turmoil and pain. Naturally, this makes it difficult to leave the relationship.

Does any of this resonate with you? Did you enter a relationship that wore down your sense of self, or had you already endured events that eroded your self-esteem prior to a toxic partnership? Perhaps this section doesn't apply to you at all, but it's still worth knowing that low worth can be exacerbated by predatory people. Many people with low self-esteem have fallen foul to a manipulator who took advantage of their vulnerabilities, and sadly, many of those individuals remain in that toxic situation.

Root of Low Self-Esteem #4: Poor Educational Performance

I wasn't particularly academic, although nor did I struggle too much at school. I was a "specialist subject student," as one of my teachers put it. If I liked a subject and wanted to know more, I'd excel in it, like I did in history and art. If I had no interest in the subject and struggled to grasp it, I'd flop at exams and get D's for my homework. Math and science come to mind when I think of the subjects I couldn't get on board with.

As a result, I was put in a "special" science class to ensure I'd hit my target end-of-year grades. The kids in that class ranged from those who had no interest in school to those who had learning difficulties. One girl in this class stood out to me. She seemed intelligent, was quiet, and did her best to grasp what the teacher was trying to get us to comprehend. No matter how much he explained or how many different ways he explained it, she never quite got what he was trying to teach her.

This would cause her a great deal of distress. She would sometimes leave the class with tears welling up, and it was clear she felt stupid, particularly when she was singled out to answer a question she couldn't find the answer to.

I would rarely get the questions correct either, but the big difference between me and this girl is that my self-esteem didn't rest on my academic performance. I knew I was good at some things. I drew pictures at home, always liked to read about anything and everything, and accepted I got A's in subjects I liked and D's in subjects I didn't. My feelings of stupidity never correlated with education. For this girl, though, her entire sense of self hung on her grades.

This is the same for many people who suffer from low self-esteem. As you know, when you feel stupid, the portal to low self-worth opens, and it's so easy to get sucked in. For so many individuals, school brings back memories of being behind the other students academically, being made to feel defective because they couldn't pick things up as easily as their peers, and dreading the teacher handing out homework at the end of the lesson. Their school days are filled with memories of feeling dread, feeling dumb, and unable to speak up and ask for help.

If there's no support from home or any parental help, then the student, in this instance, is left to deal with feelings of worthlessness on their own.

On the flip side, if the student has parents who place a great deal of emphasis on their grades, this can also open the door for low self-esteem to creep its way in. My mother always insisted I had reasonable grades. If I got mediocre results, I'd get an eye roll and was told I didn't apply myself enough. But, again, I excelled in art and creative things, and this was where my passions were, so her comments didn't consume me. Some parents, though, take grade chasing to extremes.

They withhold love and affection if their child doesn't achieve grades they deem acceptable. They punish their child for getting subpar results on their tests. They shame their child, making them feel as if their poor results reflect badly on them as a parent. As a result, the child feels responsible for the parent's disappointment and upset.

This conditional love dangled over the child creates a breeding ground for toxic self-talk, insecurity, shame, guilt, and rejection sensitivity. Aka, low self-esteem. No excellent grades = no love because they haven't earned it. They don't deserve love - they aren't worthy enough.

These children grow up to be people pleasers, full of internalized belief that they must earn the right to be loved. They're self-conscious, secretive, and refrain from sharing their honest opinions for fear of people disliking them.

Again, I want you to refer back to the notes you made from the previous chapter, where you noted down specific times your low self-esteem has made you feel shame or insecurity or caused you to talk to yourself in a toxic way. Do any of these scenarios tie back to your performance at school? Does your quickness to embarrass stem from a time you felt humiliated in class? Do you harbor feelings of shame that began in childhood after showing your parents exam results they were displeased with?

If you can, try to follow the invisible thread you're creating in your head and follow that negative emotion to its origin.

Why Do the Effects of These Situations Stay With Us?

Why do these traumatic events shape us for such a long time, often decades after they occurred in the first place? Why can't we shake them off and gain strength from these instances?

In life, we are molded by the things that happen to us and around us. When a lot of these things are negative, such as prolonged mistreatment by parents or bullying, this shapes our "core belief" of ourselves. We end up truly believing we are stupid, useless, don't deserve kindness, or that any kindness given to us is done out of pity.

Eventually, our core belief is that we are undeserving. It dictates what we do, how we do it, and what we avoid. It creates our rules for life, a rigid set of behaviors we must carry out, or we end up exposing ourselves as the pathetic, useless, broken individual we believe we are. The rules the core belief systems lay out differ from person to person, but here are some of the ones I had.

"I have to avoid criticism - if I can make my boss happy, I'll be okay."

"I will do everything to make my partner happy, even if it means sacrificing things that make me happy. That way, I'll be okay."

"I will do everything I can to avoid rejection. I'll only speak up if I know what I say won't divide opinion. That way, I'll be okay."

"I will put myself down before someone else does. This will let them know I'm aware of my flaws and don't pose a threat to them."

"When I think people are talking about me, I'll act like I don't hear them instead of acknowledging their conversation. That way, I can pretend I didn't hear it, avoid confrontation, and I'll be okay."

The list went on. The rigid rules I had created - subconsciously - served to ensure I was "okay." The biggest irony for me - and possibly for you - is that I wasn't "okay." I was far from it. These short-term solutions, created by my internal defense system to help me avoid further trauma, only served to prolong my agony of enduring life instead of living it.

Our brains are amazing, complex machines, and they do their best to shield us from difficult emotions and anxiety-provoking scenarios. When we endure enough trauma, our brain tries to stop further damage by creating these rules. And for a short while, these rules do work. They give us freedom from putting ourselves in uncomfortable situations. They mean we get to avoid rejection. They allow us to keep our spouse happy and therefore, avoid their criticism.

But you can't live your life this way long term. If you do, you're destined to endure a life of low self-worth, living just to please others and avoid confronting things you find difficult.

This is how the cycle goes:

Prolonged trauma creates your core belief system.

Your core belief system creates its own rules for living.

These rules spawn avoidant, negative, and unhelpful behavior from you, to stop you from being retraumatized from things that have affected you in the past, i.e., being rejected by a parent.

This subsequently triggers internal self-talk of a toxic nature.

So, the cycle repeats and repeats under the guise of getting you through each day. But you have to stop the cycle eventually, and you start that by entering Stage Three: tackling negative self-talk.

Before we enter the next chapter, I want you to use the correlation you've been making between childhood instances of low self-esteem triggers and your current self-perception to fuel your healing journey. I needed you to make the connection yourself. Simply telling you that your low self-worth was born out of the maltreatment of others simply wouldn't be effective enough. You need to face the trauma before defeating it.

Now, let's begin looking at how you talk to yourself.

Defeating Negative Self-Talk

Negative self-talk is deafening.

It's the devil on both of your shoulders, telling you just how awful you are, validating all the guilt and shame you feel about yourself. It affirms that how you feel about yourself is how you *should* feel about yourself.

The thing about negative self-talk, though, is it can often appear rational. It's almost as if it's your voice of reason, simply trying to help you. To stop you from making a fool of yourself. To prevent you from doing something that will cause you to land flat on your face. To save you from embarrassing yourself.

"You're not clever enough to apply for that job; don't put yourself through the humiliation of rejection."

"Your co-workers are only inviting you for lunch because they feel they have to. Decline the invite. It's a pity invite anyway."

"I'm so stupid. Why did I speak up just then? I made a fool of myself."

These toxic thoughts appear under the guise of self-preservation. To stop you doing something "stupid" or reprimanding you when you do something "stupid." Negative self-talk's disguise of helpfulness and rationality is believable.

Your inner dialogue isn't supposed to be like this, though. It may feel like you've lived this way for so long that the toxic inner talk can't possibly change, but you have to remember that you can override this toxic dialogue you have with yourself. Over time, you can rewire your thoughts to prevent cruel self-talk.

Everybody has an inner dialogue. For those with a healthy inner voice, this helps them process their thoughts in a logical, well-rounded way. For those with an unhealthy inner voice, it distorts reality, making you focus on perceived flaws and fueling judgment of yourself.

Simply put, a healthy inner voice serves you. An unhealthy inner voice sabotages you.

Negative self-talk rears its ugly head during conversations while trying to sleep at night, while you're cleaning up after dinner, before leaving the house... there's no set time or event that triggers your cruel inner critic from voicing their toxic drivel. This means it's an enemy that can pounce at any time, any place, anywhere.

There are three main types of toxic self-talk: Individualization, Disastrous, and Filtering. I'll explain what each one is before I discuss how you can tackle them. These three types of inner talk all intertwine to create one terribly toxic environment in your head - a place where you spend all of your time.

Toxic Self-Talk Type #1: Individualization

This type of self-talk sees you blame yourself for everything that goes wrong. You don't use reason, logic, or compassion when talking to yourself. You dwell on how much of a "failure" you are. You berate yourself for being useless in social situations. You chastise yourself for upsetting your partner, blaming yourself for making them mad or upsetting them. After all, you can't do anything right. Not according to your inner voice, anyway.

Individualization causes you to put a lot of unnecessary and unwarranted blame on yourself. You bear the burden of things that are out of your control, things that aren't your fault, or things that others have done.

We don't view it quite that way, though. When we blame ourselves, at least we can process the ill feelings we're having: bad things are happening, but it's all your fault, right? In your mind, trying to make sense of it all, you now feel like you have some kind of control over the situation. You're the one causing the problems, it's your fault, you're the one who caused this, you're the one who can make it right.

This is our mind's misguided way of trying to ease our inner turmoil. In reality, it just perpetuates the toxic way we speak to ourselves.

Toxic Self-Talk Type #2: Disastrous

This type of self-talk was a big one for me. I always thought of the worst-case scenario in everything I did. From a decision I made at work to the outcome of speaking up for myself, I would worry about things that hadn't happened or things that could happen. If you're like this, catastrophizing everything, just remember 99 percent of what you worry over will never materialize.

I know you're most definitely a disastrous thinker if your immediate thought is, "What about the remaining 1 percent?"

Living in this constant state of being on edge is not good for your well-being. You know this without me telling you, but sometimes we need a reminder of these things. Negative self-talk that focuses on the worst-case scenario ensures you're living life in survival mode. I say living in survival mode; I mean *enduring* life in survival mode.

You're in constant fear of losing your job, of your partner leaving you, of being abandoned by your best friend... whatever your specific disastrous scenario is, you're just waiting for it to happen. You question your every decision, afraid it's taking you one step closer to that catastrophic situation you're dreading.

What this does is paralyze you. It takes away your autonomy. Living in fear of what has not yet - and likely never will - arrive isn't living. If it does, and that 1 percent becomes reality, you deal with it. You get through it. The constant rumination and worrying over it prior to it happening didn't do anything to help, did it?

Toxic Self-Talk Type #3: Filtering

Filtering is where you process information, be it things someone has said to you, a situation you were involved in or something you've witnessed, and only retain the negative aspects (if there were any). You filter out the good or positive parts, only hearing the doom, gloom, and negativity.

For example, your partner may tell you that they like your outfit today. You should wear green more often, they tell you. You don't hear that they think you look good. You hear that they think you usually don't look good and are trying to subtly point that out.

Another example could be your boss telling you they're impressed with your productive week, but they point out an error you made while working so hard. You don't hear the praise for your hard work; you only hear the mistake you made and dwell on that aspect of the interaction.

Filtering breeds the mindset of, nothing good ever comes my way, life is a struggle, and nothing I do can change that. It breeds a victim mentality, and you become a self-fulfilling prophecy.

Challenging Negative Self-Talk

You can overcome toxic self-talk, but first, you must challenge your negative self-talk.

Challenging your toxic talk isn't all that hard - it's the consistency of doing so that is. You need to persevere with facing your inner critic when it rears its mean little head and refrain from shrugging your shoulders and going, "I guess you're right," and accepting yourself talking to yourself in a cruel way.

Let me guide you through the six steps you take mentally to battle negative self-talk.

Be Aware of Negativity Toward Yourself

It sounds like a redundant step - *you're already aware you're talking negatively to yourself.* But this initial step goes much deeper than just acknowledging it. The next time you think to yourself, "I'm such an idiot. Why did I do that," or "All I do is make mistakes. I'm so stupid," I want you to halt right there. Acknowledge how you've just spoken to yourself.

Take the negative comment you've just handed yourself and analyze it. What was the thought, what triggered it, how does it make you feel, and what's the outcome of talking to yourself that way?

By taking this time to refrain from taking your self-talk as gospel truth, you're subtly rewiring your brain to think about how you're talking to yourself. Over time, being aware of how you're talking to yourself becomes second nature, and the toxic thoughts are fully vetted before they enter.

Imagine yourself working in passport control. You check each passport, ensuring the person handing you theirs is who they say they are. If there's something amiss, you'll question the individual, and if it turns out they're not telling the truth, you turn them away from the flight they're trying to board.

That's the exercise you need to be carrying out with your toxic thoughts. There's no way to stop negative thoughts from appearing - just like you can't stop the person in the above scenario from appearing at the airport and trying to board a flight. You can, however, question them and stop them from boarding the flight, just like you can stop your toxic thoughts from consuming your mind.

Challenge the Negativity

Following up on the first step, you might wonder how to combat your unwanted thoughts. When you challenge a negative thought, a lot of the time, you're challenging an ingrained belief you have about yourself. That you're awkward, stupid, useless, or unworthy. Whatever your irrational beliefs are, they've been cemented in your thought pattern for likely years. I know it can be hard and feel difficult to challenge this when it's all you've known for so long.

These toxic beliefs that were drummed into you can be overridden. Once you've caught the toxic talk seeping through in step one, you can challenge the thought and reframe it.

For example, you may think, "I'm not clever enough to get this right." Hold it right there. Take the thought and analyze it. You're having this thought because you feel you might struggle to do something, and your ingrained belief is telling you that you won't because you lack the smarts to do so.

Reframe it from a negative thought to a helpful, positive one. "I'm not clever enough to get this right" becomes "I'm going to try and do this, and my best is all I can do." The first thought serves no purpose but to sabotage you. The second empowers you to pull your boots up and do your best. There's no talk of stupidity or not being good enough.

Another example is you overanalyzing why a work colleague is unfriendly towards you. "What have I done for them to dislike me? Perhaps I said something to upset them. I'm always saying stupid things." Stop this in its tracks. Analyze it. Reframe it.

"Perhaps I said something to upset them. I'm always saying stupid things," becomes, "I've not knowingly upset my co-workers, and if they dislike me, there's nothing I can do to change that. I will remain cordial toward them regardless and focus on things I can control."

All you're doing is changing the lens from which you look at things. Then, you're using this to reframe the way in which you talk to yourself. It is a simple yet undeniably effective way to stop negative self-talk. While it's simple, rewiring your brain takes time and consistency, so you need to practice this regularly. Of course, the odd sliver of toxicity will creep in from time to time, but as long as you can acknowledge it for what it is, you're still on the right track.

Positive Self-Talk

This is yet another simple thing to practice - in theory. As you know, talking positively or highly of yourself doesn't come naturally. In fact, we resist it, pushing it away as if we'll burst into flames if we dare indulge in such egotistical thinking. For so long, our low self-esteem has ensured only negative thinking ruled the decisions we made and the way we viewed ourselves.

So, for this step, we'll ease in gently. One day, you'll be able to acknowledge all the great things you have to offer, and your inner beliefs won't dare challenge those thoughts because they, too, will be able to acknowledge all your great attributes. For now, though, your positive self-talk will begin with just positive thoughts.

For example, I woke up this morning and was thankful that I had functioning legs that allowed me to enjoy walking the dogs. I had money in my bank that allowed me to enjoy a coffee on the way back. I was able to have a warm shower and enjoy the feeling of being clean. I had ingredients in the fridge that allowed me to prepare a casserole and share the leftovers with my three terriers.

I've just described my normal day off to you, but instead of telling you I walked the dog, took a shower, and made food, I reframed it in a positive way. By thinking with gratitude and positivity, you're setting a precedent that you don't think on a low frequency - you think on a high one.

I'd like you, starting now, to pick up this way of thinking. Don't dwell on the negative; be grateful for the positive.

I began thinking this way when I was at my lowest, and when I learned about high and low vibrations, I shrugged it off as self-help nonsense. But I had nothing to lose, so I gave it a go. Bear in mind, at this point in my life, I was struggling to pay my bills. I had chronic pain. I was worrying about how to cover next month's bills and put food on the table every day. It was easier for me to dwell on the things that were going wrong than the things I ought to be grateful for.

But I gave it a go. When I got into bed on a night, I would think how nice it felt to have clean bedding. When I raced to get the bus to work, I began thinking how grateful I was for the ability to run at will. I began with little acknowledgments of positivity here and there, and pretty soon, it became infectious.

This one little shift in my thinking really did change my life. I know that's a big statement, but gratitude really did help me break free from the tight grasp of negative self-talk.

Third-Person View

When you're engulfed by toxic self-talk and find it's consuming every fiber of your being, pause for a moment and step outside of yourself. Look at yourself from a bird's eye view, and instead of sitting there thinking poorly of yourself, imagine that it's the person you love most in the world. Your mother, partner, child, grandmother... whoever it is for you, imagine they are sitting where you are, cruelly tormenting themselves. Berating themselves, speaking to themselves with venom and dislike. Calling themselves stupid, ugly, and worthless while feeling hopeless that this negativity will ever cease.

How does that make you feel? Do you want to hug and comfort them and tell them they are worthy and loved? I imagine you do. You'd want to let them know how wrong their thoughts are and remind them that they shouldn't dwell on their shortcomings since we're all human and we all have them.

Why don't you treat yourself this way when the toxic thoughts become too much? Why would you let yourself become engulfed in the flames of toxicity without stepping in to save yourself?

Next time this happens, step out of yourself and take stock of how poorly you're treating yourself. Empathy, encouragement, and compassion take you much further than self-berating, mean words, and negativity.

Talk

This next one wasn't overly applicable to me since I had no strong familial connections, and I was unable to talk to my spouse about how I felt. However, if you can, I strongly implore you to reach out to loved ones or friends and open up about how you're feeling.

Since I'm now in a much healthier state, I can attest to the healing power of speaking up and not holding toxicity in. Secrecy and suppression only serve to fuel low self-esteem; getting how you feel out into the world is one of the biggest extinguishers for negative thoughts and toxic ruminations.

At the time I was enduring crippling low self-esteem, I had no solid connections (or felt I could trust those around me), so I kept it all in. Until I read about journaling. You may not want to keep a journal, be unfamiliar with the term, or see it as simply keeping a diary. It's more than that - it's a way of getting your thoughts out in a cohesive, clear way.

Should you wish to journal, you can even do this on your phone: all you need is ten minutes every evening to write down your feelings for the day. There are no rules except to use the word "I."

For example, this is one of my entries:

I got up early since I struggled to sleep, so I've been tired today. Hopefully, that means I'll sleep tonight. My lack of shut-eye made me grouchy in the office, but I tried to stay upbeat. This has made me worry about coming across as cold today, but I know how others perceive me isn't something I can let consume me. Overall, it was a productive day: I enjoyed making lasagne for dinner, cleaned up the spare room, and watched an episode of Grey's to unwind.

It's just a recap of my day, nothing fancy. Short, simple, and written just for me. I'd felt a bit flat that day and didn't feel like talking much at work. I didn't know why until I sat down at the end of the day to journal. By writing things out, you can get a clearer view of your thinking and unscramble your mind.

Shelve it for Later

You are in control of your thoughts. You choose what you let in, what you don't, and what you put aside to unpack later. Shelving a nasty, particularly harmful thought doesn't mean putting it to one side and letting it fester. You're boxing it up, placing it on your "To Be Unpacked" shelf, and getting on with your day.

Imagine your bedroom all cluttered, with clothes, shoes, and rubbish all over the floor, and you're trying to rummage through to find your outfit for that day. Work starts in 45 minutes, and you're flinging things around furiously, desperately searching for the clean clothes you need to put on to leave the house. In your way, however, are piles of unwashed sweatshirts, perfume bottles, towels, and spilled makeup. You're up against a total mess.

What if you took a breath and began piling the dirty laundry up and putting it to one side? You placed the make-up back in its rightful place and put the perfume back on its stand. The towels are folded back on the rack. The mess on the floor is cleaned up, and you've found your outfit. You know you have a pile of laundry to do, but it's put to one side to deal with later. You can leave the house calm, ready for the day, and in control of your thoughts.

Shelving your negative thoughts is much like this. You place it to one side to have space for clear, logical thoughts instead of fuzzy ones triggered by toxic thinking.

When you're in a position where you can't deal with a toxic thought right now - be it while you're in a meeting, talking with a friend, or in an interview - you have to shelve it. You need clarity. To be distracted by negative thinking when you need your mind to be clear and coherent, you're doing yourself a great service by shelving toxic thoughts.

The best time to declutter this shelf is on an evening when you're journaling. For me, this is the best time to unpack your day. Just remember to do so - don't let those toxic boxes on the shelf pile up, or the room will be overrun by those cartons filled to the brim with poisonous thoughts.

Now, let's begin Stage Four: tackling unnecessary guilt and blame.

Banishing Blame and Guilt

Do you feel perpetually guilty? Does it keep you awake at night or cause you to zone out randomly throughout your day? Sometimes, we feel guilt for no particular reason or can't pinpoint the reason. We feel guilt just for existing.

Sometimes, we can pinpoint the reason. Perhaps someone has done something nice for us, and we feel guilty about it. Perhaps we feel we've let someone down, and we ruminate over how awful a person that makes us. We let guilt and shame consume us, torturing ourselves into a state of unworthiness.

In small doses, guilt is, believe it or not, a healthy emotion. To be void of the ability to feel guilt or culpability is actually a psychopathic trait. We need guilt; it serves as a moral compass, guiding us into making the right choices and doing the right thing. It serves as an inner punishment for when we invariably mess up or do something that hurts someone we love. In small doses, it's healthy.

Small doses being the key component here. For those dealing with self-esteem issues, there's no such thing as a small dose of guilt or shame. It's more like an overdose of the feeling, one we cannot come down from.

When confronting the overwhelming feelings of guilt that consume us every day, there's one thing you need to remember: nobody can make you feel guilty without your permission.

It's a sobering thought, one you perhaps don't believe to be true just yet. But *I don't choose to feel guilt,* you may be thinking. Let me dive deeper into this, and by the end of this chapter, I'd like to have accomplished two things:

For you to understand your guilt.

For you to understand how to combat your feelings of guilt and shame.

First, let's look at how guilt works. Guilt comes from either a past event that you can't stop thinking about or a future event yet to happen that you're worrying over. The symptoms this emotion evokes include anxiety, being on the verge of tears or crying, inability to sleep, lack of concentration, and being withdrawn.

There are physical symptoms of guilt and shame, too, just like there is with trauma as a whole. These include being tense, being exhausted, and even dealing with frequent upset stomachs. When you're dealing with low self-esteem and all the myriad of symptoms, it can be hard to remember what it feels like to be "normal." When you're in the throes of battling low self-worth, all you want is to feel okay; you don't dare wish for all the happiness in the world because you feel you don't deserve it. Any ideas of happiness and abundance are swiftly crushed by your feelings of guilt and shame. *How dare you want more!*

You may know where your guilt complex came from. In most cases, it stems from childhood, but not always.

Children who are frequently made to feel "bad" or like they've always done something wrong quickly develop a guilt complex. The adults or caregivers, usually a parent, who instill this into the child tend to be emotionally abusive. The child learns that they make their parent or caregiver stressed, upset, and angry, and as a result, harbor constant feelings of guilt. This persistent cloud of shame remains into adulthood and only disperses once the adult confronts the root cause of their relentless guilt. (Which is what you're doing by reading books like this one.)

Shameful feelings that are born during childhood can also begin as a byproduct of living with suppressive parents. For example, a young person may feel overwhelming shame and guilt for having feelings toward someone of the same sex due to their upbringing. The parents' beliefs have been instilled into the child, and by not following their tenets, the youngster would feel like they'd failed their caregivers. They know that if they opened up to their parents about their newfound feelings, they'd be made to feel shameful. This leads to secrecy, which is one of guilt's biggest propellers.

Violating or not following cultural norms can also make a young person feel guilty. Parents do not always instill this negative emotion into a child; it can come from peers and childhood friends. When I was heading to high school, I still had dolls and toys on display that I loved when I was younger. They comforted me, and I didn't want to hide them in a box under my bed.

However, when I made a friend in my new school and invited her to my house one weekend, she saw my collection of toys on my shelf and lined up on my bed, and laughed. She couldn't believe I still "played with toys" at my age and couldn't wait to return to school the following Monday to tell everyone.

Sure enough, that Monday night I returned home and boxed up each and every "kiddy" item I had in my room. Most of it I threw out. Some items that I just couldn't bear to part with ended up in the attic. Fueled by shame and guilt for being such a big baby, I closed a chapter of my life I wasn't yet ready to close.

While this wasn't the catalyst for my feelings of guilt and shame - my mother had instilled those emotions into me much earlier - it did reinforce and fuel my constant feelings of guilt. When we feel like we're being judged, like we're not good enough to fit in, and like we can't be ourselves to be liked, we are left with frequent guilty thoughts.

At its core, the emotion of guilt comes from how your actions affect those around you. Sadly, when we are mistreated and made to feel like we're always doing something wrong, guilt can manifest into something more sinister than the moral compass it was designed to be. It becomes a mutation of a once-healthy emotion and begins to affect day-to-day living negatively. Each variation of guilt has a name. "Good" guilt is called "Adaptive Guilt." "Bad" guilt is called "Maladaptive Guilt."

Adaptive is the type of guilt that we learn from, the healthy type that corrects our mistakes, ensures we never want to repeat the same errors, and allows us to move on from wrongdoing after a little self-correction mentally. The phrase "no mistakes, just lessons" comes to mind. Adaptive guilt also helps us develop empathy and compassion for others and ensures we maintain a life that avoids purposefully hurting those around us.

Maladaptive guilt is the evil twin. The feeling is essentially the same as adaptive guilt but a hundred times more intense, a thousand times more irrational, and infinitely more self-sabotaging. Along with negative self-talk and the heightened sensitivity to rejection, maladaptive guilt serves to run your self-worth into the ground.

But how can you tackle something so ingrained? Before I cover this question, I want to remind you of something: it is entirely within your power to control your thoughts. I want you to repeat this to yourself because I know you're dubious about this statement.

It is entirely within your power to control your thoughts.

If I say something twice at any point in this book, please know it's because what I say is a key aspect of overcoming low self-esteem. For reference, I'll list them at the end of the book for you to refer to moving forward.

Defeating Guilt Step One: Identify Your Triggers

Delve into your feelings of guilt and shame. It's uncomfortable, I know, but really think about what makes you feel guilty. Be clear and honest with yourself - remember, secrecy only feeds guilt. Confront some of the reasons you feel a sense of shame about yourself, take yourself back to times when you've felt immense guilt, and think about what triggered it. Perhaps you can even recall the first time you were made to feel guilty.

Ruminate for a while about your triggers: what brings on feelings of guilt?

As I mentioned, guilt is healthy in small doses. The things that cause you to feel guilt and shame, are they warranted? In other words, are you responsible for what you feel guilty or ashamed about? Or, as is often the case for people living with low self-esteem, are you feeling guilty over something you have no power over?

Things you have no power over include what other people think of you, how other people treat you, other people's actions, and the past... in fact, it's probably easier for me to tell you what you do have power over: your thoughts, your feelings, and your actions.

Defeating Guilt Step Two: Introspection and Self-awareness

Introspection is defined as "the examination or observation of one's own mental and emotional processes." There has to be a good amount of introspection with intent when you're battling low self-esteem. Once you break through the discomfort, you become a whole new level of self-aware.

With that in mind, when you begin to feel overwhelmed with guilt and shame, consider confronting your feelings. When you're feeling guilty over "could haves" or "should haves" or feeling shame over how people judge you, ask yourself some important questions:

Are these thoughts and feelings based on what other people expect of you?

Are these thoughts and feelings brought on by how others value you?

More often than not, our negative feelings and self-loathing aren't brought on by a genuine reason to feel guilty. It's the childhood you, still hurting inside of you, feeling those immense feelings of guilt and shame. When you feel judged, misunderstood, like a disappointment, and like you're less than, you regress to the shame-filled child inside.

If this resonates with you, consider writing down how you feel. Before you think *I'll skip this section*, please hear me out. I get it; writing things down might not be your thing (if it is, then you may have begun this next exercise already). Please, stick with me. Even if afterward, you wish to destroy the paper your feelings are on, the act of writing your feelings out can help you rationalize and process them. In fact, destroying the pain-filled pages you write could be a therapeutic, cathartic way of signaling to yourself that you're ready to get rid of them.

If you're averse to writing things down, either because you don't want the notes to be found by others or simply because you don't think you can get your muddled thoughts out coherently,

I implore you to give it a go. Grab a clean sheet of paper. Now, I want you to write out the answer to the following question: in a word or short sentence, what is the most current thing you feel guilt or shame over?

Be specific, don't be general. Don't write "work" or "relationship" - these are vague generalizations that don't hone in on the true source of your feelings. Then, write a description of how this makes you feel. Let your feelings spill onto the page: upset, angry, misunderstood, anxious, needy, unable to cope, overwhelmed... whatever words that describe how you're feeling, note them down.

Now, examine the feelings of guilt more thoroughly. You can identify the person or situation that prompts these feelings; now, let's break down *why* this makes you feel full of shame and guilt. What factors helped contribute to how you're feeling? Are you placing your value as a person on other people and factors you can't control?

If there was an instance that you feel you could have handled better, consider refocusing your guilt from maladaptive to adaptive: you know you could have done something differently, and you'll do so in the future. Don't keep berating yourself; it only keeps you in the cycle of guilt and shame.

Write down everything you're processing about your excessive feelings of guilt. You can keep it for future reference to see how far you've come, or you can rip it to shreds as a symbol of your commitment to overcoming your negative feelings about yourself.

Defeating Guilt Step Three: Self-compassion

Would I be wrong if I said that you consider yourself a compassionate, empathic person? Those of us who suffer from self-esteem issues have often been through enough to feel deep empathy for others. More often than not, we are empaths, able to tune in to the emotional vibrations of those around us. If a loved one is hurt or upset, so are we.

Why, then, does this compassion not include yourself? Ponder this question for a moment. Why do you offer so much thought, concern, and empathy for others but cannot give yourself even just a fraction of that consideration?

One of the most important things you can do throughout your journey to conquer low self-esteem is to practice self-compassion. It's not self-indulgent or egotistical; it's a key component of a healthy mind.

You need to treat yourself like your best friend. You naturally become your best friend when you obtain a healthy view of yourself. You're compassionate and you validate your feelings but also keep yourself accountable where necessary. You never talk down to yourself, you don't torture yourself with toxic put-downs, and you don't refer to yourself as stupid or undeserving. Just like you wouldn't with a friend.

Imagine yourself duplicated, and there's a copy of you sitting next to you right now. One filled with knowledge, compassion, understanding, comfort, and rationale. View yourself from their eyes when considering your negative feelings toward yourself. They're sitting beside you, watching you treat yourself with utter dislike and malice. How does this make you feel?

What would a friend do when they see someone they care about struggling mentally? Would they tell them they're right to feel persistent guilt, overwhelming self-loathing, and insecurity? You need to remember that you reside in your mind for your whole life. Why make it full of hatred toward yourself?

There are three main components to self-compassion. First is acknowledging that you're human and will do things you wish you hadn't (no mistakes, just lessons, remember?)

That's okay. What's not okay is treating yourself poorly because you messed up. Everybody messes up; it's what makes us human. There's never been a person in history who hasn't made an error of judgment, done something stupid, or done something regretful. Think of someone you admire, a celebrity, or even someone you know. Whether you know about it or not, they've messed up in their life. They've made bad calls, and no doubt they've done things that have upset another person. Does that make them a bad person to you? Of course not.

You have to allow yourself room for error.

Next, you must maintain the mindset of treating yourself like you treat those you love and care about. Empathy and offering understanding are important aspects of caring about someone. Offer yourself that in abundance, too.

Remember, toxic talk has no place in your brain, just like it has no place when you're talking to anyone else. Be your own caregiver.

In thinking this way, you open up a world you had no idea existed: one of self-acceptance. When you embrace your shortcomings or perceived "flaws" without overkilling your thoughts with toxic self-talk, you're in a much better position to rationalize. You can accept you have weak areas - as all humans do - but you don't let them define you.

When you're in the trenches of low self-esteem, you are defined by everything you think is wrong with you. Take the power away from this toxic thought cycle by acknowledging your weaknesses, accepting them, and not magnifying them. Don't be full of harsh judgment toward yourself - remember to treat yourself like a friend.

Finally, you need to change your perspective. Or, rather, regain perspective. You'll know yourself that your self-perception is skewed. Who can blame you, with all that self-berating and critical self-talk swarming your thoughts? But now you've gained knowledge and more awareness about the way you talk to yourself. You can offer yourself the ability to gain a new perspective on yourself.

You've acknowledged your flaws and agreed with yourself to be kinder moving forward. What about all your good points? You have them. You've just neglected to acknowledge their existence in favor of ruminating over your weaknesses and imperfections. When you shift perspective, you can view yourself in a more holistic way as a complete person with good aspects, weaker traits, quirky qualities, and everything else a human being embodies.

A solid self-perception also helps us erode our need for outside validation. You may be just like I was, desperate to be liked and only ever spoken of in a good light. This is an impossible pressure to put on yourself. Not everybody will like you, and not everybody will see all your great characteristics. You can't control this. But I know this doesn't stop us from feeling deflated and devastated when we find out someone dislikes us or talks about us unfavorably.

To help you look at the bigger picture, get your pen and paper out again. Draw a line down the center of the page and headline the left side "control" and the right side "no control." Fill each column out, writing down the things in your life you have control over and the things you don't. I'll wait here while you do that.

On the left-hand side, you should have:

My thoughts.

My feelings

My actions.

On the right-hand side, you should have:

Everything else.

There are few things in the world we can control except ourselves. When we acknowledge and accept this, it's a freeing realization. With that in mind, ask yourself what good there is in upsetting yourself over things you can't control? All that does is serve to keep your self-esteem at rock bottom.

Defeating Guilt Step Four: Affirmations

Affirmations aren't as woo-woo as some people would have you think. You don't need to sit and chant them - although you can if you want, and I can't deny doing it myself in the past. In fact, it can be a good morning routine to stand in front of the mirror and say your chosen affirmation aloud five times. If you choose to say them to yourself in your head, that's fine, too. The main point is that you're affirming these statements to yourself to be true.

You deserve to live a life of mental peace and clarity and to feel deserving of good things. You might be thinking, I don't truly feel that way about myself. Or, you may agree you want to feel that way, but it seems an unobtainable feat for you. The way you get there is by affirming it. Reminding yourself every day that you are worthy.

These affirmations can be anything, but let me give you a template for what an affirmation ought to be. You can use the ones I suggest here if you find them applicable, but amend as needed:

I release unwarranted guilt, shame, and embarrassment.

I will show myself kindness and compassion at all times.

I am a good person and deserve to heal from my traumas.

I will not focus on the past or future but focus on today - the here and now.

Even if you don't believe in the power of affirmations, give this a go. Aim to begin doing it every day for a week. You're not just telling yourself these affirmations; you're telling your subconscious. Your subconscious doesn't know the difference between sarcasm, jokes, or self-deprecating humor - it takes everything literally. When you remind yourself daily that you're worthy, important, and deserving, you'll soon find your pattern of thinking pulling away from the same old toxic thoughts that have plagued you for so long.

Don't carry guilt and shame around with you. It doesn't serve you; it sabotages you. You are the only one who can fix that. With that in mind, let's move on to Stage Five: toxic comparisons and imposter syndrome. Just like all the guilt and shame you harbor, negative comparisons to others are feelings many of us deal with. However, throwing poor self-perception into the mix can make social comparison a dangerous thing to engage in.

Social Comparison and Imposter Syndrome

Comparing yourself to others is a natural behavior. Stripping it back to basics, much like low doses of guilt, social comparison aids us in day-to-day life. We learn from others, their shortcomings, and what they excel at. We can use others to show us what's possible and to gauge how to navigate certain situations. It helps us keep up with our potential.

Social comparison can become unhealthy, though, particularly for those of us who struggle with viewing ourselves as worthy individuals. It becomes the imp sitting on our shoulders as we scroll social media or watch television, telling us we're lesser than because we're not as pretty as the person on TV or as fit as the influencers on social media. We become fueled by self-loathing, stressed that we aren't where we "should" be in life, and waste precious time worrying about where we are compared to others.

You'll notice a common theme throughout this book: childhood. Most of the things we deal with as adults begin as childhood trauma, and social comparison-related trauma is no different. Unlike abusive mothers or cruel bullies, though, social comparison is a requirement. It's in our DNA.

Refer back to being a child. Your friend just got a new game console, and you still don't have one. You get upset that they're seemingly better than you: they have the coolest new fad, and you don't. Then, you head to school, and another friend is wearing the sneakers that are currently in fashion, and you're stuck with last year's footwear. These feelings are natural, and the comparison is juvenile.

However, you might have dealt with some more social comparisons during your childhood that affected you long-term. Perhaps your mother unfavorably compared you to your sibling or made you feel "less than" them. Maybe your parents told you they wished you were more like one of your school friends who got good grades and was academic. Perhaps you were made to feel less pretty or attractive than your peers, with cruel jibes still haunting you to this day.

These are the situations where toxic social comparison is born. It goes far deeper than just wanting to "fit in" or have cool things. Your very core is being attacked, as are the things out of your control. Your academic skills, your looks, your personality, and your capabilities. No wonder these pressures manifest into self-loathing toxicity.

Let's look at the two types of social comparison: upward and downward.

Upward social comparison

This sees us look to those who are in a perceived "better" position. This could be someone living your dream career, a friend in a seemingly loved-up, perfect relationship, or an acquaintance traveling the world - something you'd love to do. We look at these individuals for inspiration, hope, and verification that these things are attainable. However, when we engage in upward social comparison, our feelings can go one of two ways: we can feel happy for the person living out our goals and use them as inspiration. Or, we can feel envy, jealousy, and unfairness about it, and toxic thoughts swarm our minds.

On the other end of the spectrum, there is:

Downward social comparison

This is where we refer to those we feel are in a worse position than us. We do so to make us feel better about ourselves and our own situation. As cruel as it sounds, when you're desperate to know you're not "that bad" , you seek that kind of validation from dubious places.

For example, you might be insecure about how you look or have feelings of ugliness. You might use someone else as an example and tell yourself, "At least I don't look like that!"

For someone with low self-esteem, this downward compassion will help dampen their feelings of not being good enough - but only for a short time.

It's no surprise then, that your self-esteem determines how you deal with social comparison. For a healthy person, the comparison isn't toxic; it's motivational. For those with low self-esteem, it serves as an added stressor to an already negative self-view. When self-worth is at rock bottom, everything can be seen as a threat, from the pretty model on TV to the neighbor driving a brand-new car. It's a horrible way to live and doesn't serve any practical purpose.

This brings me to a huge detrimental factor in social comparison: social media.

Having some kind of social media is unavoidable at this point. This means viewing perfect people living perfect lives is also practically unavoidable. It can be hard to believe that the snapshots we see online aren't real; lifestyles are frequently faked, selfies are often edited, and happy poses can hide unhappiness beneath the veneer. Still, we compare our lives to the curated moments people put online. Bear in mind, people don't post "just woken up" selfies or disagreements with their spouse online (*for the most part, anyway!*)

They don't post their toddler meltdowns, their poor performance reviews at work, their low bank balances, their strained relationship with their parents, their partner's infidelity, the 45 photos it took before getting the "perfect" one... you only get the rose-tinted, filtered images that the individual wants you to see.

Why would you compare your life as a whole to somebody else's highlights?

Everybody has their own path. No two paths are the same. That makes comparing yourself unfavorably to someone else fruitless for you.

If you can acknowledge you indulge in social comparison in a negative way, you're halfway to overcoming it. Truthfully, at one point or another, we've all engaged in toxic social comparison. If you feel yourself doing it, there are ways to nip it in the bud before it consumes you.

Firstly, you can reframe how you're viewing the recipient of your social comparison. Instead of comparing yourself in an unfavorable way, look to that person as inspiration and motivation. Oh, they've traveled to four countries this year? You'd love to travel, and one day you're going to embark on something similar. Perhaps they've secured a promotion in a role you want. Again, use this as fuel for improvement, not fuel for negativity.

If you find yourself harming your emotional well-being by consuming social media and comparing yourself harshly, then you need to recognize this as a potential trigger for your negative, self-berating thoughts. Consider taking a break from social media while you work on building your self-esteem.

If you don't wish to take a break, streamline your social media feed. Unfollow accounts that trigger you to ruminate about how worthless you believe you are. Make an effort to follow accounts that trigger positive feelings in you. Curate your feed as if it were your mind; only allow in what you invite in.

Similarly, if it's someone in real life who triggers your inner critic, such as a friend who brags about their lifestyle, you may consider limiting your exposure to them while you're working on yourself. If you must compare yourself to someone, make it your past self. That ought to be the only person you're up against.

After all, if you're using other people as your benchmark of success and happiness, you're letting them decide what you want in life.

Social comparison ties in with impostor syndrome, something that affects just about everybody who's ever dealt with low self-esteem. The term is used to describe the feeling you get when you believe you are a fraud in a successful situation.

For example, you may feel like a phony at work, believing you only got the job because you lucked out at the interview, and now you live in fear of being "found out." You may feel like you're a fraud in your relationship, believing your spouse has chosen someone well below their league and are waiting for the day they'll discover this. Any area of your life that can be seen as impressive, you may feel like an imposter - as if the spot you filled was made for someone else, someone "better."

Imposter syndrome is complex, just like most aspects concerning the knock-on effects of low self-esteem. It's not diagnosable, like low self-esteem, but it certainly exists. Here are some signs that you're dealing with imposter syndrome:

You attribute your success to things out of your control, i.e, luck or someone taking pity on you.

You struggle with constructive advice - you feel like this exposes your lack of knowledge.

You're scared people can "see through you" - as if you're going to be uncovered as a fraud.

You obsess over tiny mistakes you've made.

You may even label yourself as a "perfectionist," but really, you have to excel at any given area; otherwise, you feel others will expose you for the phony you feel you are.

Living with imposter syndrome is tiring, and if you can relate to any of the above statements, you'll attest to this. You're a constant ball of anxiety, doing your best to hide your biggest secret: that you're not good enough, and fighting to hide that fact from everyone.

Of course, that's not true - the idea that you're not good enough is simply your internal negative belief system striking again. But that doesn't make it feel any less true, and as a result, you're left suffering in silence, trying to stay afloat in a pool you don't feel you deserve to swim in in the first place.

One of the most frustrating things about imposter syndrome is that no matter what you do, how many barriers you break through, or how hard you work to achieve something, you'll always feel undeserving. You'll diminish your hard work and effort and call it "luck."

So, where does imposter syndrome begin? Where could such a horrible thing be created? Are you thinking: *childhood experiences*?

If so, you'd be right. You can't process your successes because you've been made to feel like you're not good enough. Even with evidence presented to you suggesting otherwise, you simply can't internalize it. Critical parents, hurtful bullies, or disinterested caregivers' treatment of you has created an adult who simply can't accept they're worthy of good things.

In order to combat this, let me ask you some questions. You can think about the answers or write them down. Either way, the answer is for you. All I'm doing is holding the mirror up to you; you're the one producing all the answers here.

Do I have to be perfect to be deserving?

Was my inner belief system molded by people who mistreated me?

Why do I choose to overlook my strengths in order to focus on my weaknesses?

If I were to try to overcome imposter syndrome, what would I be losing by doing so, and what would I gain from doing so?

Take your time in answering those questions. Your answers are likely longer and more complex as you delve into them.

As you consider social comparison and imposter syndrome and the effects they have on you, Stage Six awaits you: asserting yourself without feeling pangs of guilt for doing so.

Assertiveness Without Guilt: Setting Boundaries

It's a sad truth that those with low self-esteem also have low barriers when setting personal boundaries. We let ourselves be used, give so much of ourselves to others for fear of them disliking or abandoning us, and let others override our decisions to suit their own wants.

If you're unfamiliar with boundaries, essentially, they are the rules you have for yourself that determine how you're willing to be treated. It's an invisible bubble we have around ourselves, and that bubble encompasses all the behaviors we find unacceptable from others. For example, one of your boundaries can be that you will not accept being lied to. Another can be that you don't want to be contacted after 10 p.m. at night. It could be that one of your boundaries is that you will not tolerate being spoken to in an aggressive manner.

We all have boundaries, but those with low self-esteem are much less likely to enforce those boundaries. So, you may tell yourself, I will not accept my partner coming home late again this week after I told them I was making dinner, and they agreed to be home by 7 p.m. When 7 p.m. comes and goes, and the dinner is cold, you are upset and angry that your partner let you down. It's already happened a dozen times this year despite you telling them how much it hurts you. They've agreed to be more mindful and be home on time when they say they will.

Yet again, though, they've not regarded your boundary. After all, there is no repercussion for the disrespectful partner - you won't leave them. You won't tell them how deflated you feel. You won't reiterate that you respect their wants and needs and expect the same in return.

For someone with healthy boundaries, they would not put up with persistent disrespect. They'd offer their partner the chance to make amends, prove they respect their spouse's boundaries and agree to consider their partner when making decisions. Should the spouse keep flouting these boundaries, showing a lack of care for them, and breaking promises, a person with healthy boundaries would likely remove themselves from that situation.

But where do unhealthy boundaries come from?

You've probably already got the answer: childhood.

More often than not, we've been molded to bend and shift our own wants, needs, and desires to ensure other people are comfortable. My earliest childhood memories of having my boundaries dismissed was me being made to give my grandfather a kiss. "Go on, you're upsetting your Grandad; go kiss him now!" was my mother's response to my refusal to embrace my dad's father. I wasn't close to this side of the family and had only ever met my grandfather a handful of times. Every other time I'd have to peck him on the face, he would give me a hug that squeezed my tiny frame and hurt me. I simply didn't want to give the man a kiss, but that didn't matter - I was made to. If I didn't, I caused upset, disappointment, and, more memorably, I caused people to dislike me.

This is how it begins, and it spirals from there. The demolition and dismissal of your boundaries may have begun differently. Perhaps you desired to wear a comfy sweater and sneakers to school, but your mother overrode your choice and made you wear a dress you felt uncomfortable in. Maybe you wanted to take the creative writing class, but your father insisted you take something more practical. If you didn't, you'd upset him and cause him a great deal of stress. Wherever your weak boundary setting began, the result remains the same: people are still able to cross those boundaries with little to no pushback.

And who can blame us for carrying this into adulthood with us? It's become our mechanism for survival, to keep people happy and avoid hurting and upsetting those around us. We've learned that in order to get by, we have to have weak border control with our boundaries. We let just about everything and everyone pass. If we dare enforce these boundaries, we simply don't feel able to deal with the upset it'd cause.

This way of thinking, though, entirely neglects the fact that by doing this, we're putting everybody else's needs above our own. We're shaving off pieces of ourselves to give to them, eventually leaving nothing but a husk.

It's not healthy not just for you but for the people who trample over your boundaries, too. Having weak boundaries doesn't aid anybody in living a healthy, mindful, happy life. You may know yourself, but letting others violate the rules you have in place leaves you feeling full of disdain, discomfort, and anger. You feel stuck because you hate being violated, but you also don't feel able to call out those who dismiss the clearly labeled boundaries. You don't want to be seen as rude, self-important, or uptight.

For a healthy mind, you must set boundaries. Repeat that: for a healthy mind, you must set boundaries.

Let me show you how you can strengthen your boundaries and assert your requirement for your needs to be met. You may feel uncomfortable thinking about putting these things into practice, but if you don't, all you're ever going to be doing is sacrificing your own needs in favor of other's wants. By enforcing boundaries, you're not creating unhappiness for others or depleting their happiness for your own gain; this is a common misconception that you need to quash right now.

You are setting boundaries to create respect, trust, and positive communication. You respect others' boundaries, and so you expect the same in return.

You might be struggling to understand what your boundaries are anymore. When you feel this way, a trusty pen and pad (or your phone) can be a good way to get the details from the fogginess of your brain.

Your list may look like this:

I will not be told "no" when I ask for some space. I ask for space because it's something I need to maintain a healthy mind, this will not be something I forgo any longer.

I will no longer accept shouting as a form of communication. Shouting and aggression aren't behaviors I will tolerate.

I will not be made to do things I say "no" to and will not do things against my will to appease those around me.

These are items from my own list of boundaries that I set out years ago. I thought I'd already been enforcing these things, but upon writing them down, I realized that I'd never verbally communicated them. You may, probably correctly, assume that these types of boundaries should always be adhered to without them being vocalized. However, some individuals need assertive reminders that boundaries are there for good reason and should never be dismissed.

If that person gets upset with you setting your boundaries, you need to remember this: people who are upset when you set boundaries are the same people who benefit from you having none. Let me repeat that because you may need to refer to it again in the future to remind yourself:

People who are upset when you set boundaries are the same people who benefit from you having none.

Setting Boundaries Tip #1: Get to the point. I get that you may feel uncomfortable doing this. You've spent so long not doing this that it doesn't come naturally. So, rambling and unclear communication can be the result. You need to verbally set boundaries in a clear, straightforward manner and ensure they've been understood.

You don't need to raise your voice, get upset, or unleash years' worth of pent-up frustration out on the recipient. Be calm, clear, and concise.

Setting Boundaries Tip #2: Use direct language. If you ramble and go on a tirade about how you hate it when your spouse disregards your feelings and you are sick to death of asking time and time again for their respect, you may lose sight of the goal you have. You may end up making the other person become defensive if you come across as attacking.

All you need to do is clearly and directly state your boundaries. Once this has been received, you can have a more in-depth conversation about the events that have led to you speaking up for yourself. Until then, you need to ensure there is no way your boundary setting could get lost in translation.

Setting Boundaries Tip #3: Embrace the discomfort that comes from doing this. You only get uncomfortable when you do things outside of your comfort zone, and as the saying goes, nothing good ever happens there.

You will feel pings of awkwardness and may even second-guess what you're doing. Stick with it - only through this discomfort can you come through the other side and reclaim your right to having self-worth.

I know you may be left with guilt or feeling shame for setting boundaries. Remember, this is non-negotiable for those with a healthy view of themselves and others. If someone dislikes your boundaries, you need to question why that would be.

Feeling remorse over setting basic boundaries is common for those of us who were made to feel selfish or bad for expressing our needs by our caregivers. But you can't let old feelings rule your life forever. Having weak boundaries comes from surviving toxic environments. Maintaining this poor standard only keeps the cycle of toxicity going.

Assertiveness without guilt comes down to this: expressing yourself openly and in a respectful manner. You do not list out demands - after all, you cannot control other people's actions, nor should you try. You're asking to be listened to and for your needs to be respected. You are not being accusatory or starting an argument by outlining your boundaries.

Ask yourself: *why should you feel guilty about this*?

You might be thinking to yourself, I've tried setting boundaries before, and I'm still in the same position as before.

Maintaining boundaries is just as important as setting them. Let me guide you through ways that you can uphold these non-negotiables after verbalizing them and clearly setting them out.

Maintaining Boundaries 101

When you're first starting to set out your boundaries or are struggling to maintain the ones already verbalized, then strip it back to the bare bones. Begin with a few non-negotiables and build from there.

Successfully maintain one boundary: for example, your boundary is being able to read a book in an evening without being spoken to for an hour. You work to maintain this and remind those around you that you're going to take an hour of your time to unwind. If someone interrupts or calls your phone, you reaffirm the boundary. This shows you that you can commit to what you've put in place.

Take things slowly and at a pace that suits you. The more you can keep your boundaries in place without allowing people to disregard them, the more confident and comfortable you'll be managing other boundaries you may have.

Ideally, you set boundaries early on in a relationship. This doesn't make or break your ability to set and maintain boundaries, but it's something to keep in mind when making new friends or new colleagues. If you set out expectations early on, nobody can feel confused later on.

One of the big things you need to keep in mind when maintaining boundaries is consistency. In fact, consistency as a whole is important to overcoming low self-esteem. The key thing is, no matter how much easier it may feel to let expectations slide or how much simpler it is to let people disregard your boundaries, you have to reinforce them should the situation require.

Letting things slide and not being consistent in enforcing your non-negotiables blur the line for you and the person crossing your boundary. They get away with it once; they're going to assume they can get away with it again. Avoid this confusion by remaining consistent.

If and when your boundary has been crossed, you need to gently remind the person who has done so that you have firm boundaries in place for a reason. This can be challenging for us people-pleasers and those afraid of conflict but don't view it as a confrontation. What many of us called "confrontation" for years actually turned out to be healthy communication.

So, using the example above of requiring an hour of reading time in the evening. Should your partner interrupt you or someone is blowing up your phone, you must communicate your boundaries.

You'd say something like, "I know you want to chat, but since I'm in the middle of my reading hour, the best thing to do is wait until 7 p.m. when I'm free." It's gentle yet effective in reminding people of your boundaries and lets the offender know you're no longer willing to bend your needs to meet their wants. Keep reinforcing your boundaries, and those around you will get to understand your threshold.

Consistency and gentle reinforcement go a long way in being assertive without feeling guilty.

If there's one section of this chapter I want you to remember when asserting your boundaries, it's this phrase: "No" is a full sentence. I'll say that again, and this time, think about what it means: "No" is a full sentence.

So Important, I Say it Twice

Thank you for reading *The Low Self-Esteem Struggle*. I appreciate you taking the time to read and digest this book. There's a lot to unpack when you're tackling your low self-esteem. It's important to remember that the journey from feeling hopeless and not good enough to realizing your worth doesn't happen overnight.

It takes consistent checking in with any toxic thoughts that creep in. It takes daily reminders to be gentle with yourself and treat yourself like a friend. It takes inner strength to shift your self-perception and acknowledge and accept your flaws.

This book isn't a hefty tome filled with scientific talk trying to assess the correlation between the hippocampus and low self-esteem. When fighting my own battle with self-esteem, I sought refuge in books on the subject, and plenty of them were filled with jargon I simply didn't understand. All I wanted to know was why I felt the way I felt, how I could overcome those feelings, and know that feeling worthy was within my reach. I just wanted the tools to find my worth, not the science behind my lack of it.

I hope this book is different. I hope it has succinctly and clearly given you an uncomplicated explanation of low self-esteem and given you a set of mental tools to use in your battle to overcome it. There aren't 300 pages to flick through, no fluff, and no jargon. Simple, actionable advice from someone who's been there. I truly hope my intent of making this book compact and actionable and making the content within obtainable has come across.

As I mentioned in one of the earlier chapters, I would repeat some of the "so important, I'll say it twice" quotes. Bookmark the page, type the quotes out, or write them down; whatever you do, refer back to them when you feel lost.

"No" is a full sentence.

Low self-esteem is not a personality trait.

For a healthy mind, you must set boundaries.

It is entirely within your power to control your thoughts.

People who are upset when you set boundaries are the same people who benefit from you having none.

Thank you so much for reading,

Scout

P.S. You can join my upcoming newsletter about *The Self Struggle* here:

ScoutAddison.carrd.co[1]

---

1. http://scoutaddison.carrd.co